AF505004

Puppy Training

A Step-by-Step Guide to Crate Training, Potty Training, Obedience Training, and Behavior Training

Julia Chandler

© Text Copyright 2023 by Julia Chandler - All rights reserved.

This document is geared towards providing exact and reliable information in regards to the topic and issue covered. The publication is sold with the idea that the publisher is not required to render accounting, officially permitted, or otherwise, qualified services. If advice is necessary, legal, or professional, a practiced individual in the profession should be ordered.

From a Declaration of Principles which was accepted and approved equally by a Committee of the American Bar Association and a Committee of Publishers and Associations.

In no way is it legal to reproduce, duplicate, or transmit any part of this document in either electronic means or in printed format. Recording of this publication is strictly prohibited and any storage of this document is not allowed unless with written permission from the publisher. All rights reserved.

The information provided herein is stated to be truthful and consistent, in that any liability, in terms of inattention or otherwise, by any usage or abuse of any policies, processes, or directions contained within is the solitary and utter responsibility of the recipient reader. Under no circumstances will any legal responsibility or blame be held against the publisher for any reparation, damages, or monetary loss due to the information herein, either directly or indirectly.

Respective authors own all copyrights not held by the publisher.

The information herein is offered for informational purposes solely, and is universal as so. The presentation of the information is without contract or any type of guarantee assurance.

The trademarks that are used are without any consent, and the publication of the trademark is without permission or backing by the trademark owner. All trademarks and brands within this book are for clarifying purposes only and are owned by the owners themselves, not affiliated with this document.

Table of Contents

Introduction 1

CHAPTER ONE 3

Puppy-Proofing Your Home.......................... 3

    Poisonous Plants... 3
    How to Puppy-Proof Your Home 5

CHAPTER TWO 8

Useful Puppy Training Tips........................... 8

    Be Consistent 8
    Treats and Training 10
    Communicating Your Intentions Clearly 12
    Be Patient 12
    Clicker Training 13
    Training Yourself 15

CHAPTER THREE...17

Leash Training for Puppies..........................17

    Choosing a Collar 17
    Choosing a Leash 18
    Introduce the Collar 20
    Introduce the Leash 20
    Learn to Walk on the Leash 21

CHAPTER FOUR...23

Crate Training for Puppies..........................23

    Buying a Crate.. 23
    Crate Training Steps 24

CHAPTER FIVE **29**

Potty Training Your Puppy **29**

Wait Until Your Puppy Is the Right Age 29
Potty Training Tips 30
How to Handle Accidents 32

CHAPTER SIX **34**

Obedience Training for Puppies **34**

Obedience Training: Teaching to Heel.....................36
Obedience Training: Teaching to Sit...................... 38
Obedience Training: Teaching to Stay 40
Obedience Training: Teaching to Come...................41
Obedience Training: Teaching to Lie Down.............41
Obedience Training: Teaching 'No' 43

CHAPTER SEVEN **46**

Behavior Training for Puppies **46**

Nipping and Biting 46
Digging.. 48
Train Your Puppy to Not Bark............................. 50

Conclusion **53**

Introduction

A puppy is a fun companion who turns into a loyal and devoted friend as he matures. When he is separated from his natural family, all he wants is a new one that he can love and that will provide him with food and shelter. That new family will be you. The quicker he learns the rules of his new home, the happier both of you will be. A puppy usually wants to please, and it's up to you to show him how to live in the world.

Training your puppy will help your new friend to understand what is expected of him and to gain confidence. Proper training will also strengthen the bond between you and your puppy and make it possible for you to include your puppy in your daily activities more often. A well-trained puppy is a happy, well balanced puppy, and of course that's what you want for your new best friend.

This book will make puppy training a whole lot easier for you. The book features proven methods and step-by-step instructions for training your puppy and introducing him to your home, your visitors, and the general public. Chapter 1 introduces how to puppy-proof your home, and Chapter 2 provides you with useful puppy training tips. Chapter 3 shows how to begin leash training and Chapter 4 explains crate training. Potty training is one of the most important tasks when a puppy comes home and this is covered in Chapter 5. In addition, Chapter 6 introduces the best way to teach your puppy obedience commands. And finally, Chapter 7 contains tips on how to stop destructive behaviors.

With patience and consistency, your new puppy will learn what he is supposed to do and you will be well on your way to building an extremely satisfying, lifelong friendship that will be more rewarding than you ever thought possible.

CHAPTER ONE

Puppy-Proofing Your Home

Congratulations! You have found your dream puppy. Before that fluffy bundle of fur bounces through your front door, there are some preparations to do.

Puppies are full of energy; they are curious and love to explore. This makes them fun and lovely, but can also lead them to harmful situations. Before you bring your puppy home, make sure you survey your home and remove potential dangers to provide a safe environment for the new member of your family. Puppy-proofing your home is similar to preparing your home for a toddler.

Poisonous Plants

Some plants are poisonous and dangerous if your pup ingests them. A few common plants that you need to be aware of include:

Azalea: Eating just a few leaves of the azalea plant can be dangerous to your dog. It can cause diarrhea and vomiting.

Daffodils: Ingesting either the plant or the bulb can result in abdominal pain, diarrhea, and vomiting.

Lily of the Valley: These can cause severe cardiac problems, seizure, diarrhea, and vomiting.

Autumn Crocus: The autumn crocus is severely toxic and can cause respiratory failure, liver and kidney problems, and gastrointestinal bleeding.

Cyclamen: If ingested, this plant can be fatal to your dog.

Oleander: The leaves and flowers of this garden shrub are toxic when ingested.

Dieffenbachia: This plant can cause nausea and vomiting.

Tulips: It's the tulip bulbs that are toxic, so make sure your dog doesn't go digging for them in your garden.

These are just a few of the plants that are a real danger to your dog. Check with your veterinarian or Pet Poison Control for a complete list.

How to Puppy-Proof Your Home

Indoors

- Don't leave coins lying around – metal can poison or choke your puppy.

- Never leave chocolate where a puppy can get it – chocolate is toxic to dogs.

- All medications and vitamins should be kept out of the puppy's reach. Never keep pills on the counter, table, or dresser. Your curious puppy can easily chew through a plastic container, and will happily do so if given the chance.

- Everyday cleaning supplies should be kept out of puppy's reach or behind childproof locks. Also, keep in mind that while you are cleaning, toxic vapors can get into the puppy's eyes and lungs. Your puppy should be kept in another room.

- Puppies love to chew on electrical and cable cords, which can cause burns or electric shock. You can buy cord concealers or protective cable wrap to keep your electrical cords and your puppy safe.

- Never leave CDs or DVDs lying around. A puppy can chew them into sharp shards, which will do some serious damage.

- Bathtubs and sinks filled with water are a potential drowning hazard. Also keep the lid on your toilet.

- Space heaters, fireplaces, or candles should never be left on when your puppy is alone in a room, even for a minute.

- Put any sentimental or precious items out of puppy's reach. Even if they're not toxic, you want to be sure your puppy doesn't decide some beloved old photograph is a fun chew toy.

• Never leave food lying around. Alcohol, chocolate, coffee, onions, and sugar can cause serious problems to your puppy's digestive system. Tobacco, smoking patches, and nicotine gum can be fatal if ingested. Be aware that food scraps, such as chicken bones, coffee grounds, or uncooked meats can be a health hazard to your puppy.

• There are puppies that mistake cat feces for food! If you have a cat, keep its litter box separated from the puppy by using a baby gate.

Outdoors

• If you have a yard, your puppy needs to be in a fenced-in area or an outdoor kennel to keep him from straying and investigating the neighborhood.

• **A** swimming pool is a real problem. You could put a cover over the pool until your puppy is old enough.

• Be sure to block any access to a shed or garage that contains insecticide, gasoline, paint, oil, or fertilizer. Your puppy will actually like the taste of rat poison or antifreeze, which can be fatal.

CHAPTER TWO

Useful Puppy Training Tips

From your puppy's point of view, you are the alpha dog. It's up to you to keep your new puppy safe and protected, and to help him establish boundaries. Here are some puppy training tips you can use to teach your puppy everything he needs to know to start the journey of becoming your very best friend.

Be Consistent

Your puppy is eager to please you, but he can't always tell right from wrong. He can't read your mind. A puppy's world can get very confusing, and it is up to you to provide immediate positive reinforcement for good behavior and absolutely no reward for bad behavior.

Dogs need to experience the consequences of their behavior immediately. They will work hard to get what they want and to avoid what they don't want. But they need to understand the consequences between behavior and result. If you give your puppy a treat fifteen minutes after he followed your "sit" order, he will be happy, but he will have no idea why he's getting a treat. There is no connection between the "sit" and the biscuit, and it will have no bearing on future behavior. Immediacy and timing are crucial.

The same is true for withholding rewards. If your puppy behaves badly, you should hold the treat so that the puppy can see it, but do not give it to him. If you don't give him a treat fifteen minutes later, it is much too late to serve as negative reinforcement. Remain consistent in your own behavior, and your puppy will quickly learn cause and effect.

Keep in mind that no reward is not the same as punishment. No reward means withholding something your puppy wants. Getting punished confuses him. He understands that you are upset, but he's not clear why. Your puppy is unable to reason. But if you withhold a treat, the cause and effect of behavior becomes clearer.

Establish routines with your puppy, such as regular feeding times, walk and play times, and bathroom breaks. Stick with your routines and this will help speed up the process. Be consistent since inconsistencies will only confuse your puppy and prolong the training process.

If you don't want your puppy to jump on people when they come through the front door, you need to reinforce that expectation every time. Allowing the pup to jump all over your sister but not your neighbor will cause confusion. Use the "sit," "stay," or "heel" command to get your puppy's attention and do it every time.

Treats and Training

Everyone, including puppies, loves treats. You can use these as a reward for good behavior. Dog treats come in all flavors, sizes, and specialties. Soft, meaty treats are very enticing to most puppies, and having a ready supply will help your puppy quickly learn what behaviors are wanted and rewarded. Puppies usually love anything cheese, peanut butter, or meat flavored. Select small treats instead of big ones that require lots of chewing. The trick with training is to use quick, positive reinforcement and small, bite sized treats are perfect rewards for your puppy.

Drop a treat into the crate in order to lure your dog in there. Provide a treat anytime the puppy goes to the bathroom outside or sits and rolls over when commanded. Don't give your dog treats for no reason, or this will confuse the situation and they won't realize they're being rewarded. Make sure it's a specific dog treat that you're providing as well. You might think ice cream makes a great treat, but it's not so good for your puppy.

Communicating Your Intentions Clearly

There's nothing wrong with explicitly telling your puppy "no," only that it often fails to offer enough information. Instead, you can tell him what you want. Dogs don't usually generalize well, so if the dog jumps on someone in excitement and you say "no," he may jump higher or change direction. A better alternative would be to instruct him to sit. Telling him what you want helps to avoid confusion.

Focus on simple commands. Your puppy doesn't understand English, and when you say, "Sit down, Fido!" "I want you to sit!" or "Come on, sit!" all he hears is a jumble of confusing words. Repeating the word "sit" will help your puppy associate that sound with the desired behavior. Use a single word instead of a sentence or phrase, and use that word consistently.

Be Patient

Don't allow yourself to get frustrated or impatient during the training process, with yourself, or with your new puppy. It will take some time to accomplish all of the goals you have set for you new pal, and for you to get the hang of your puppy's unique personality, likes, and the techniques and rewards that work best for your puppy.

Give your puppy time to understand new commands. He most likely won't learn it the first couple of times when you teach him. Repeat old commands in new training sessions, so that he doesn't forget them. The attention span of dogs is pretty short, so keep your sessions frequent but short in length, otherwise your pup will become bored.

Work on simple commands before moving on to more complex behaviors. For example, if you want your puppy to sit and stay, first work on the sitting, then the staying, before doing both. If your puppy is having difficulty, you may be moving too fast. Take a step back and start over.

Never get impatient with your puppy and never call him to you if you are going to punish him – all that will do is teach him that to come to you is not a good thing. Keep your voice firm but gentle, and never let any frustration creep into it.

Clicker Training

For many puppies, a clicker is a great tool for training. Small and inexpensive, clickers work by capturing your dog's attention with an audible sound. Simply press the clicker's button when your puppy does what you want him to do and follow the click with a positive reward, such as a small treat or an enthusiastic, encouraging pet, a scratch behind the ears and a "good boy!" verbal reinforcement.

Training Yourself

When you introduce a new dog into your household and your life, you're not just training the puppy. You're training yourself as well. Your life is going to have to change, and you need to be prepared for it and willing to adapt. Sleeping in until noon on the weekends is no longer an option when you have a puppy that needs to be walked and fed. Taking off for a spontaneous vacation sounds like fun, but first you'll have to make arrangements for the pup. Working with the dog to be calm and quiet when friends and family visit takes a lot of energy and a willingness to hang in there for the long term.

You are working on forming a lifelong bond; be patient and consistent with the process, and it will work. All the puppy training tips in the world won't work if you have a short fuse or a lack of interest in making your puppy comfortable and behaved. Puppies are adorable, but they're also a lot of work. Before you take the plunge into new puppy ownership, make sure you're willing to invest the time, emotional energy, and resources. For specific puppy training tips, you can call on experts in the field. Pet stores, veterinarians, and fellow dog owners can all help you and your puppy become good roommates and family members.

CHAPTER THREE

Leash Training for Puppies

While playing with your puppy is fun and provides some exercise, walking your puppy is the best way to help him expend pent up energy and calm his mind. Though some puppies are initially wary of wearing a collar and a leash, these leash training tips will have you proudly walking a well behaved, happy pup sooner than you ever thought possible.

Choosing a Collar

A collar is a functional accessory that your dog will wear around his neck. The collar can attach to a leash or a harness when it's time to go for a walk and it can also be used to hold any dog tags or documentation that you received when you registered your puppy. There are collars on the market that can also be used to train your dog and instill good behaviors. Small dogs do well in a harness so they can't slip out of their collars. Harnesses can work well for puppies of all breeds.

When you are gathering your supplies, buy items that can grow with your puppy. Collars should be adjustable and checked frequently for a proper fit. Your puppy will grow quickly and you do not want his collar to be too tight or uncomfortable. When fitting your puppy's collar, be sure that you can fit two fingers between the collar and his neck. This measurement will ensure that the collar is snug enough to keep your puppy secure, but won't be tight and uncomfortable. When you're shopping for collars, make sure the collar you select has a sturdy metal ring to attach the leash to when you begin to leash train and walk your puppy.

Choosing a Leash

The leash accompanies the collar, especially if you don't have an outdoor space where your puppy can run free. It might seem like walking on a leash should be second nature to your puppy, but it's actually a learned behavior.

Look for a leash that is secure and fits well on the collar or the harness you're using. When selecting the first leash to use for your puppy, pick one that is lightweight. A heavy leash may add pressure to the puppy's neck and make leash training more difficult than it needs to be. Give the puppy enough leash space to roam around independently, but not so much leash that the dog can run into traffic or get into trouble. Retractable leashes are often a good option because you can decide how long the distance should stretch between you and your little buddy.

Introduce the Collar

When you first introduce the collar to your pup, be sure it fits properly. Make putting the collar on fun by using an upbeat, but calm voice and reward your pup with a treat once the collar is fastened. Some puppies will try to push the collar off or scratch at it, after all it is a new sensation! If your pup does this, distract him with a toy, a treat, or scratch him behind the ears. Anytime you see your pup messing with his collar, apply a positive distraction, and soon your puppy won't even notice he's wearing a collar.

Introduce the Leash

Once your puppy is used to the collar, it's time to introduce him to the leash. Select a lightweight leash so there is no unnecessary pulling that may make your puppy leery of the leash. Clip the leash onto the collar and call your puppy to you. Some puppies will have a major reaction to the leash and thrash around wildly trying to get off the leash. This is normal, so simply drop the leash and allow your puppy to pull it behind him as he wriggles, squirms, and hops. Do not let your puppy out of your sight since the leash can become caught up on something and hurt your puppy. Continue to put the leash on for short periods of time, dropping down to one knee and calling your puppy to you and rewarding him when he comes. Once he reaches you, pick up the leash and walk him short distances around the house. Repeat this a couple of times a day until your puppy is accustomed to the leash. Make the process fun by verbally praising your puppy and offering treats.

Never pull or tug harshly on the leash, fight your puppy on the leash, or yell at your puppy, as those negative behaviors will only confuse the puppy and set your training back. Be patient with your pup and keep a consistent routine of attaching the leash and letting your pup get used to it slowly and at his own pace.

Learn to Walk on the Leash

By now, your puppy is used to walking short distances inside on a leash and it's time to take the fun outside. The outside world offers lots of fun and distraction. All the sights, smells, and sounds will be new and a bit overwhelming. Even though your pup knows how to be led on the leash, he may act differently outside. If he pulls, stop and stand completely still, and do not move until he comes back to you. If he lunges at other dogs, squirrels, or other distractions, distract him with a treat or verbal command. Be patient, start with short walks at first and soon you and your pup can increase the time and distance of your walks.

CHAPTER FOUR

Crate Training for Puppies

It might seem cruel to confine a dog to a metal crate. However, crates make puppies feel safe and secure as they mimic the dog's natural den habitat. Crate training your puppy is an excellent idea, especially if you want your dog to sleep in the crate at night or you plan to be out of the house for most of the day. This protects your property by keeping your puppy from destroying your house while you are unable to supervise your puppy. It's also a way for your new puppy to feel safe. While there might be some whimpering and resistance the first time you confine your pup to a crate, the training will work quickly and your dog will become accustomed to the security of the crate.

Buying a Crate

Crates come in a number of different sizes, and you can find crates that are metal, plastic, and even fabric. When shopping for a crate, look for crates just large enough for your puppy to stand and turn around in. If your puppy will soon grow too large for a crate, look for larger crates that include a crate divider. This way, you can use the crate divider to block off half the crate until your puppy grows large enough to fill the crate space, and you avoid the expense of buying multiple crates. If you're unsure about what kind to buy, consider renting one from an animal shelter. This would work especially well for a puppy that has yet to grow.

Put the crate in your bedroom at night if your dog has separation anxiety. Many people also find that placing an article of clothing or an old towel inside the crate is a good idea; the dog will be comforted by your scent.

Crate Training Steps

Start by putting the crate in a familiar and busy area, such as the kitchen or living room. Place a cozy towel, blanket, or toy inside and leave the door open. Most puppies will follow their natural curiosity and begin to investigate. If your puppy doesn't, play or talk to him by the crate. When he's used to the crate being there, toss a few treats inside the door, then further inside. If he still doesn't go in, take a break and try again later. Keep throwing treats inside until he goes inside. Remain patient. This can be a quick process, or it can take a few days.

When the puppy is comfortable with the crate, start putting his regular food close-by. This will increase the good association he has with the crate. As soon as he easily goes inside, place his meals inside. For each feeding, move the food further inside and toward the back.

As soon as the puppy is relaxed with eating inside the crate, shut the crate door while he is eating. Open the door immediately when he is finished. Then start leaving the door shut for longer periods, until he's comfortable staying inside for about 15 minutes. Let him out if he starts to fuss and whine. You may have rushed him. Start over by keeping him inside the crate for a shorter time.

Once your puppy is used to eating inside the crate, it's time for him to get used to remaining inside for longer non-eating periods in your presence. Go to the crate and have a treat in your hand. Pick a cue word, such as "crate," "kennel," or "inside" and point at the inside with the treat. When he goes into the crate, let him have the treat, praise him enthusiastically, and shut the crate door.

Remain quietly nearby for a few minutes before going to another part of the house. You might hear barking or whining, and that's okay. Come back into the room after about 10 minutes and sit next to the crate again. Then, let the puppy out. Keep repeating this until you are able to leave the room without your puppy barking.

When you and your puppy get to the point that entering the crate is not a struggle and you can be in another room for half an hour without any barking or begging, you can probably leave the house and safely keep your puppy in the crate. Try not to be gone too long. Puppies don't have the bladder strength of older dogs, and they will need to go outside every few hours. If you are away all day long, have a dog sitter take your puppy out every few hours.

Use the crate at night as well. Keep the crate in your bedroom or close by, because the dog may need to go out during the night, and you'll want to hear the warning signs.

One thing you should never do is use the crate as a punishment. Don't put your puppy in there as a retaliation for misbehaving, barking, or biting. Crate training requires a feeling of comfort and security for your pup.

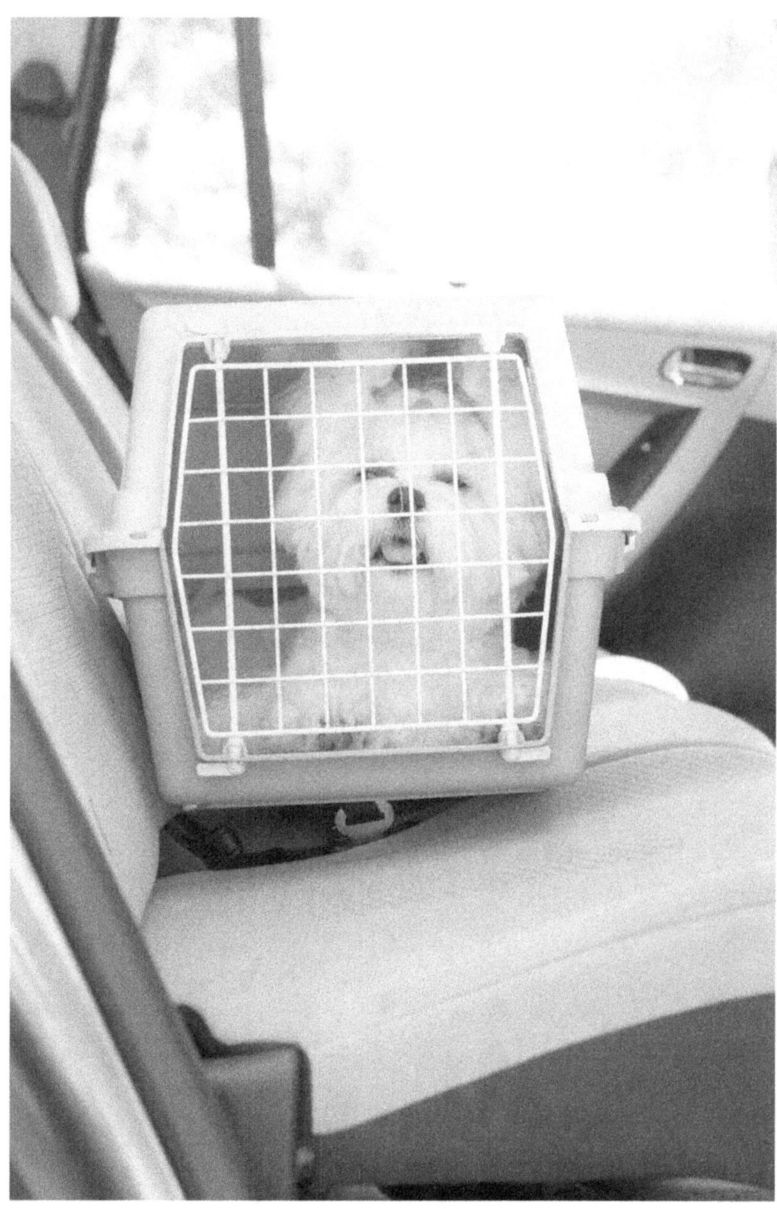

All dogs are different. You might have a puppy who loves the crate, or you might have a puppy who needs constant treats as bribes to get into the crate. If your puppy suffers from separation anxiety when crated, try having a specially favorite toy or treat that you use just for that purpose. If he receives this toy only when inside the crate, he might start looking forward to it!

CHAPTER FIVE

Potty Training Your Puppy

For many people, potty training their puppy is the most daunting part of bringing a new dog into the family. Potty training a puppy can be time consuming and messy. However, it's absolutely essential for your dog's growth and development, as well as your peace of mind. Here are a few tips to keep in mind when you are ready to begin the potty training process.

Wait Until Your Puppy Is the Right Age

Puppies less than 12-16 weeks old simply do not have enough control over their bladders to be potty trained. Hold off on potty training until your puppy is at least 12 weeks old. Until then, keep a supply of disposable or washable potty pads your puppy can use. These pads usually have a scent embedded in them that attracts the puppy to eliminate on them. If you see your puppy using the bathroom off the pad, gently pick him up and move him to the pad, then praise him for using the potty.

Potty Training Tips

Once your puppy has reached the right age, it's important to establish a potty training routine, and to be consistent and patient with it. You will need to take your puppy out immediately after he wakes up, 15 minutes after he eats or drinks, at least once an hour while he is awake, before you put him in his crate and immediately after you take him out of the crate. To help prevent accidents, be sure you keep your puppy on a regular feeding schedule and remove the food once he has finished eating, but always allow him access to water. Puppy's digestive systems are quick and efficient and taking him out 15 minutes after he eats will help get him used to going potty outside.

Puppies cannot be expected to hold their bladders all night, so you will also need to set an alarm during the night so you can take him outside. Expecting your puppy to hold his bladder throughout the night is not only unrealistic, it is a sure-fire way to ensure he soils his crate or gets a nasty bladder infection trying to hold it far longer than he is capable of or should be expected to. It is also important to watch for bathroom "tells" puppies often display. Twirling in circles, whining, scratching, and sniffing the floor are often indications the puppy needs to go potty, so if you see or hear these things, take him outside immediately.

It is also important that you take your puppy to the same spot every time to use the bathroom. Be patient with your puppy and do not try to force him, yell at him, or rush him to use the potty. Simply stand in the designated spot and use upbeat, positive verbal encouragements to "go potty" and allow your puppy time to sniff out the perfect spot and relieve himself. Once your puppy does his business, be sure to reward him with positive praise, a treat, and lots of snuggles, pets, and kisses. If he is leash-trained and enjoys going for a walk, that could be a great reward. Most puppies truly want to please their masters and letting your puppy know he is good and did the right thing will help your puppy's potty training progress at a faster rate.

How to Handle Accidents

Accidents are going to happen. Just accept accidents as part of the process and do not overreact to them. Your puppy is not being willful, disobedient, or resistant, it's simply part of the process so do not punish him by spanking him, rubbing his nose in it, or yelling at him. If you notice your pup is beginning to pee or poop in the house, clap your hands or make a loud noise. You want to startle the puppy and get his attention, but you don't want to scare the dog. Calmly say "No" and take him to his spot outside.

When an accident does occur in the house, simply clean up the accident and move on. You cannot apply a correction after the fact, the puppy will have no idea what is going on, why he is being told "No" or what he was supposed to do. Unlike humans, puppies live in the moment and once it has passed, they do not have a recollection of the accident. Trying to discipline a puppy for a past action will only make him scared and make it difficult for him to trust you. Never strike your puppy when you find accidents, or for any other reason. Hitting your puppy will only crush his spirit and break the bond you are trying to build; striking your puppy will not correct his behavior or make the process faster.

If you brought your puppy home when he was older than 12 weeks, he might have lived and eliminated in a cage. If that is the case, it may take a bit longer to house train him because you'll probably have to "untrain" a few bad habits. Don't worry. You and your pup will get there.

Be patient and consistent with your potty training routine and be gentle, kind and loving with your puppy. You'd never yell at, punish, or berate a baby for accidents, so don't do it to your dog. Follow these potty training tips and in just a few weeks, your puppy will be potty trained and you can feel good about a job well done.

CHAPTER SIX

Obedience Training for Puppies

Training your puppy to obey will open up new lines of communication between the two of you and bring you even closer. You will be able to instruct him in proper and desired behavior, and he will know what you want him to do.

Dogs are hierarchical beings and easily adapt to the social pecking order. Obedience training puts you in charge and allows the dog to show respect. Dogs usually love to perform submissive tricks such as raising a paw in a shake or licking your hand, gestures which underscores the hierarchy in your home.

Make obedience training fun for both of you. It's a great bonding experience and will make your dog more confident and enjoyable to be around. However young your puppy is, you can start behavior training now.

Begin training your puppy in familiar surroundings. Sure, you want your puppy to heel while taking a walk, but you shouldn't start training on the street. Do you want him to sit and stay in a car? Don't do the training on the highway.

Remember that puppies are young and active, so keep your training sessions short and make sure they are not hungry or tired. If your puppy, like most puppies, is constantly underfoot and demanding attention, make use of that time and teach. Have him "heel" while you go from the bedroom to the kitchen, have him "sit" while preparing coffee. This way, training becomes a part of the day.

As we've discussed, rewards for proper behavior and praise are the most critical part of training. Be sure to use real rewards. Some dogs will train for kibbles alone, but others will not. Try using bits of left-over chicken, pieces of cheese or a favorite toy to see to what your dog best responds.

Obedience Training: Teaching to Heel

Teaching your puppy how to heel is important, especially when there are other dogs around, or people that your dog might want to jump on without invitation. To heel means to walk at the side of, or next to you. When you teach your puppy to heel, he will be keeping your pace. He'll stop when you do. He'll walk when you do. This lets your puppy know that you, the pack alpha, are in charge. It's also an excellent way for the two of you to walk without a leash, when that is possible. This is a difficult thing for puppies to learn, especially since they are so energetic and curious by nature.

Use a long leash for heel training. This will give your puppy more wiggle room for mistakes and give you more chances to correct those errors. Before starting, make sure he has mastered walking with a loose leash, that is, without tugging.

The key to this part of puppy training is of course, with treats. Start by standing with your puppy on a leash and keep a few treats in the hand that isn't holding the leash. The puppy needs to understand the command, so tell your dog to heel. Once he sits still next to you for about five seconds, give the dog a treat. Then, take five steps forward and allow your do to follow. Say the word "heel" and wait for your puppy to sit down next to you. Reward with a treat. Continue doing this so your puppy understands. The dog will associate your movements and words with the expected behaviors.

Once this is successfully completed in the same location, introduce some other people and distractions. You might feel like you're starting the process all over again, but that's only because your puppy will notice those other people or bouncing balls or moving cars. Repeat the process with the treats until your dog is obedient and able to heel on command.

Obedience Training: Teaching to Sit

It's important for your puppy to learn to sit. It's the starting point for many other commands, and it's an important skill when you're outside amidst cars, at curbs or when someone is coming into your house. It's an easy command, and your puppy should master it quickly. As always, treats play the most important role.

Stand in front of your puppy and hold your hand above his head with a treat in it. He will look up at it. Use your other hand to gently push down on his hind quarters to the ground, into a sitting position. At the same time, while still holding that treat, say "sit" in a calm but firm voice. Once he is able to hold the position, give the puppy the treat.

Keep repeating this action several times each day until the puppy is able to put himself into a sitting position without your guidance. If your puppy temporarily loses the training you've mastered, simply start again. You might notice your puppy jumps on people when they come into your house or runs after children in the neighborhood. Give the command to sit, and if the dog does not listen, go back to the basics with

the treat and the physical lowering of your dog into the
sitting position.

Obedience Training: Teaching to Stay

The "stay" command should logically follow the "sit" command. After all, what is the point of teaching your puppy to sit if he doesn't stay down? Once he learns to stay, he won't lunge and jump at your guests. It will also keep him out of dangerous situations. Please keep in mind that "stay" may be difficult for your puppy to grasp, as his favorite thing is to follow you and stay by your side.

Start by having your puppy sit. After the dog is in the sit position, tell the dog to "stay," wait two seconds, and then give the dog a treat. Increase the amount of time you make the dog wait for the treat until the dog is able to wait for 10 seconds, each time, telling the dog to stay.

Each time you say, "stay," put up your hand, flat, with the palm facing the dog. This will become your hand command once your dog learns how to stay. If the dog gets up from the sitting position, say, "No," have the dog sit again, and start the process over.

When the dog is able to stay in the sitting position for 10 seconds without getting up, continue the process, but this time take one step away from the dog. Repeat the word, "stay." Take two more steps, repeat the word, "stay." Finally, step out of the dog's sight.

Continue to work with the dog until you are able to stay out of the dog's sight for two minutes without him moving.

Incorporate the "stay" command into your daily life. He may obey in the kitchen, but not in the yard or while walking, so use different situations and places to train him. Have him stay while you get the door, go through the mail, chat with a neighbor, or are on the phone. Slowly, remove the treat and continue with the hand signal and lots of praise.

Obedience Training: Teaching to Come

Puppies always want to come when they're called. They want to know what you're up to and they're eager to be close to you and a part of whatever you're doing. However, it can be difficult to get your puppy to come if the dog is preoccupied with something else. Maybe the puppy is digging in the backyard or stalking a squirrel, or completely obsessed with the scent on some random car's tires. The trick is to teach the dog that coming to you is the best decision that could ever be made.

For training purposes, call your puppy from one room to another. Stand in the kitchen when your puppy is in the living room and call your puppy's name. When your puppy comes running, get excited, pet the dog, and provide a treat. When the puppy is able to understand that coming when called means only positive things, the dog will obey immediately.

Obedience Training: Teaching to Lie Down

Your puppy should start this training in the "sit" position, so do this after he knows how to sit. Also, be careful about what cue word you use. If you use "down" to tell him get off the couch or bed, he'll be confused.

Begin with the "sit" command in an area without distractions. Make sure the floor is reasonably comfortable. Small dogs especially may find a cold, hard surface unappealing. A carpeted area is good.

When your puppy is seated, give him the verbal "down" cue. Hold a treat in your hand where he can see and smell it. Move your hand with the treat downward to the floor. The puppy will bend down to follow the treat by getting in a lying position.

Make sure his entire body is down. If you need to, lower your dog's body to the floor so the puppy understands what lying down means. If his rear end is up, he doesn't get a treat, and you start from the beginning. As soon as your puppy is lying down, give him his treat and praise him.

When he has mastered this, start using a downward hand movement without the verbal command to get him to lie down. When you do this, keep the treat hidden to allow the puppy to focus on your hand.

Obedience Training: Teaching 'No'

Your puppy needs to learn right from wrong just like an infant. And like an infant, he may choose to ignore you or simply become confused. Responding by yelling louder and louder is unproductive. The puppy hears the noise, but may have a hard time relating it to any specific behavior. This can become frustrating for both of you.

Many people combine the noise with punishment, which only exacerbates the problem.

The "no" command will ensure that you have a well-behaved and welcome puppy anywhere.

Obviously, "no" can only be taught and reinforced when your puppy misbehaves, so you'll be working on his time schedule. Keep your voice calm. Always use the same command word instead of confusing him with, "Don't do that," "Stop it now," "Get down," etc.

When your puppy does something inappropriate or objectionable, such as biting, barking, or jumping on a guest, clap firmly and say the word "no" in a strong, loud voice. You only want to say it once because you're training the dog to listen the first time. The clapping should startle and confuse the puppy enough for him to stop performing the inappropriate act.

If he stops, reward him with praise and a treat. If he doesn't stop, be firmer. Slightly stamp a foot, if necessary. (This is not the same as punishing and frightening him. It is meant to get his attention.)

If your puppy continues to misbehave, attach his leash to his collar and hold him firmly. The leash will prevent his behavior (such as jumping on people), and it will negatively "reward" him with disappointment.

When you take off the leash, if your puppy behaves, praise and reward him. If your puppy continues to misbehave, start over. Clap, say a firm no, and hold him with the leash. He'll figure out that disobedience results in not being able to run freely.

You won't be able to train your new puppy overnight. However, with time and structure, obedience training can be conquered.

CHAPTER SEVEN

Behavior Training for Puppies

Your puppy loves to investigate his world. From nipping, chewing and digging, he wants to investigate it all. In order for puppies to become well-behaved household pets, they need to be trained in what acceptable behavior is and what isn't. While it might be fun to watch your puppy acting cute, it's not fun to listen to barking, pick up scraps of what was once your favorite pair of slippers, or repair the once-landscaped backyard that has been dug to pieces. Behavior training for your puppy is absolutely necessary, for your peace of mind and your little dog's own protection.

Nipping and Biting

Your puppy naturally gets his teeth into everything; for him, it's fun. For you and your family, not so much. He can, however, learn that people have delicate skin and not to bite.

When you watch a litter of puppies play, you'll notice they love to pounce on and bite each other. This is normal behavior, and when a pup gets too rough, his playmate will yelp and stop playing. This confuses the biter, but he learns how to be gentler in his approach.

When your puppy bites, tell him "no" in a loud and firm voice and stop playing. Start to play again until he stops using his teeth. Your puppy will learn that not biting will get him playtime, while biting will put an end to playing. Keep repeating that until he knows not to hurt.

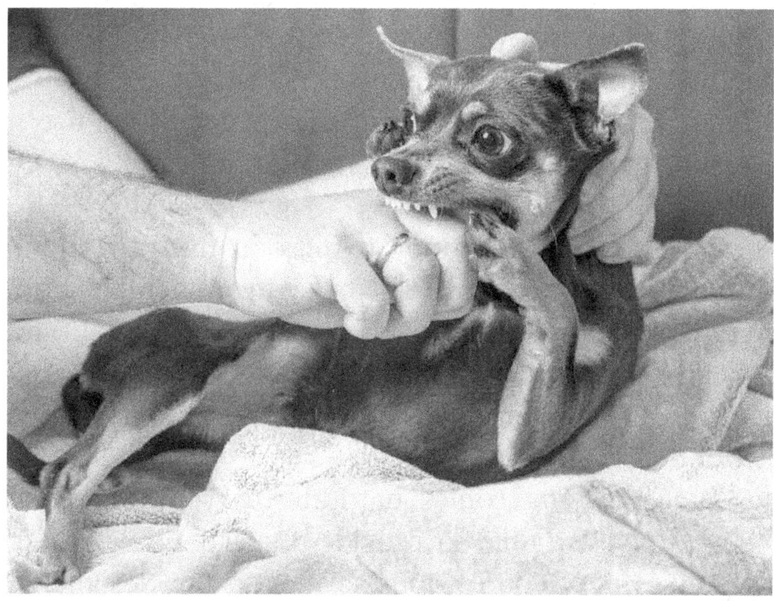

If he starts to gnaw on your finger, give him a chew toy to bite.

There are many reasons why dogs become aggressive and bite. The dog may feel over excited or that he is threatened. A lot of dog aggression comes from the lack of confidence and positive training. It is very important that you socialize your puppy with different people, dogs, children, and environments. Socialization boosts his confidence and reduces his fear in new environments. Remember to give lots of praise and treats to reward good behavior. Go see a vet if your puppy shows signs of aggression constantly.

Digging

Puppies tend to view their yard as their personal playground to be dug up and explored. They also enjoy "hiding" favorite toys. That is natural behavior, but you can teach him to restrain himself.

When you see him digging, clap loudly or use a whistle. This will distract him and let him concentrate on you.

Don't allow the puppy to play in the yard alone until he learns to control this behavior. When he starts to dig, immediately use distraction to get his attention. An excellent distraction is to toss treats around the area. He'll go after them and forget, at least momentarily, about digging up dirt.

Since digging comes naturally to your puppy, it helps if you are able to provide a specific area where digging is allowed. To confine him to the designated area, hide a few treats or toys in the digging area. Call him and let him explore for buried treasures. If he moves to areas of the yard that are off-limits, bring him back. Make sure the rewards he loves so dearly can only be found in the marked and specified area. Praise him when he digs there.

You could also discourage him from digging at unwanted places by putting small amounts of diluted pepper in the area. The best way to stop digging is to spend more play time with him and give him more activities and exercise to drain his energy.

Train Your Puppy to Not Bark

Puppies bark for a reason. If you want to control your puppy's barking, you need to understand why he barks. He may be barking at anyone walking by the house, or he may bark to alert you to someone approaching the front door. Or he may need to go to the bathroom.

Barking is also the puppy's way of expressing distress. Consider whether his environment is calm or frantic. Does he get enough exercise? If these are a problem, excessive barking is the effect and not the cause of the problem. If he barks excitedly when you come home, what he's communicating is loneliness after spending hours alone. Consider if there are factors in the dog's environment that need to be changed. Having a sitter take him for a walk and play with him during the day could alleviate some of his frustrations.

The odds are you don't want to stop your puppy's barking entirely. You certainly want him to alert you to danger, and maybe you appreciate being warned when someone is at the door. What you want to stop is barking for no reason. The better you know your dog, the better you will understand him.

One way to stop your puppy from barking is to teach him a command to bark when you want him to bark. This allows you to control when he barks and when he stops barking.

First, get him to bark while he's on a leash. If the doorbell sets him off, have someone ring it. The leash will allow you to distract him when you want to. Teach him that he can bark when the doorbell rings, but must remain quiet while you open the door.

1. When the doorbell rings, give your puppy the command to "speak." This lets him know it's okay to bark.

2. Before opening the door, show him a treat and say, "quiet." He does not get the treat until he stops barking.

3. When he stops barking, praise and treat him and open the door.

4. You should add the "sit" or "down" command so your puppy knows what he should do instead of barking.

If your puppy is barking due to pent-up energy, find ways to distract him. Usually, simply slamming something down will create enough noise to make him forget why he barked in the first place. You can also drop something, like a book, in front of him. Just make sure you don't hit the puppy.

There are bark collars that set off a noise when your puppy barks. The drawback, however, is that the collar will inhibit reasonable barking that you want, so take that into consideration.

Behavior training for puppies might seem overwhelming, but if you follow these tips, you'll have a well-behaved dog in no time.

Conclusion

If you want to raise your puppy into a good dog who knows what is expected, then you need to train him early. Initially, the puppy won't have any reason to follow your commands. Why should he stay when there's a fun world out there? Why shouldn't he steal your lunch when it's so tasty? That's how your puppy looks at it, and it's hard to argue with his logic.

That is why consistent reward and praise are so important. Rewards are the motivator to help the puppy see life your way. Training a puppy takes an abundance of patience, but the results are always worth it.

Proper training lets your puppy become a valued member of the family. Your life and his will be much easier if he knows what you expect of him. He will be welcome in more places if he can walk nicely, not jump on guests, and can keep from destroying furniture.

Training should be fun, exciting, and provide you with better means to communicate with your new family member. Start your training right away and don't give up until you have the behaviors you want from your puppy.

Finally, I want to thank you for reading my book. If you enjoyed the book, please take the time to share your thoughts and post a review on the book retailer's website. It would be greatly appreciated!

Best wishes,
Julia Chandler

www.ingramcontent.com/pod-product-compliance
Lightning Source LLC
Chambersburg PA
CBHW060225170726
48004CB00004BA/1448